Irish Coins

Written by **Dr A. E. J. Went**

Although coins were struck for use in England from about the time of Christ none were minted for Ireland until *c.* 995, when small silver pieces, in imitation of the contemporary Anglo-Saxon coins, were produced. Many of them have on the obverse a human head (**2**) and on the reverse a long cross (**1**). Some bear the name of Sihtric, the Silkenbeard, the Scandinavian king who ruled over Dublin at the turn of the tenth century, together with the name of the moneyer or person responsible for producing the coins. With the passage of time these Hiberno-Norse coins became very crude, with their legends often quite meaningless. Issues were made until *c.* 1150 and it has been estimated that no more than 2,000 specimens, most in museums, exist of this early Irish coinage.

The next issues of Irish coins bear the name of Prince John. All were rather crude coins struck in 1185 and 1198–9 (**3** and **4**). They were mainly halfpennies with a few farthings. Following these issues were the rare coins bearing the name of John de Coursy, Lord of Ulster, and later for King John a series of pennies, halfpennies and a few farthings minted in Dublin, Limerick and Waterford (**5** to **7**).

In the period 1251–4, pennies were struck in Dublin for Henry III. They have a crowned facing head in a triangle on the obverse (**8**) with a long cross with pellets in the angles. Some of these pennies were cut into halves or quarters to pass as halfpennies and farthings.

1 & 2. *Obverse & Reverse,* Hiberno-Norse, penny, 1015–35. **3** & **4**. *O. & R.* halfpenny, John as Prince, 1190–9. **5** & **6**. *O. & R.* penny, John as King, 1204–11. **7**. *O.* halfpenny, John, 1204–11. **8**. *O.* penny, Henry III, 1251–4. All enlarged in size.

Several distinct issues of coins were made for Edward I. They were mainly pennies but the last issue in the period 1296–1303 included halfpennies and farthings also. These coins were minted mainly in Dublin but large numbers of the type illustrated (9 and 10) were struck in Reginald's Tower in Waterford, and some in Cork. A few pennies were minted in Dublin for Edward III and Henry VI.

In the reign of Edward IV (1461–83) groats, 4d (11), halfgroats, 2d and pennies were minted in many Irish towns, including Dublin, Drogheda, Galway, Limerick, Trim (12), Waterford and Wexford. Many of these coins are now rare. In the short reign of Richard III groats and halfgroats were minted in Dublin and Drogheda. Some of these rare coins have on the reverse three crowns arranged vertically.

Reginald's Tower, Waterford

9 & 10. *O.* & *R.* penny, Edward I (Waterford mint), 1281–8. 11. *O.* groat (4d), Edward IV, 1461–3. 12. *O.* groat, Edward IV (Trim mint), 1465–7. All enlarged in size.

The 'three-crown' coinage was continued early in Henry VII's reign but later the obverse had a facing bust, as used earlier. Harps first appeared on the coins of Henry VIII, some having initials applicable to some of his queens (**13**). Henry's head appears on a posthumous issue of four denominations issued from 1547 to 1550 but a shilling with the young crowned head of Edward VI was issued in 1552. Base silver coins were issued for Mary Tudor before her marriage and others were struck later with facing busts of Mary and her husband, Philip of Spain. Base silver coins for Elizabeth were issued in 1558 and 1601–2 (**16**). Fine silver shillings and groats were issued in 1561 (**14** and **15**), with three harps on the reverse.

⑬	**13**. *O.* groat, Henry VIII, 1534–5.
⑭ ⑮	**14 & 15**. *O.* shilling, & *R.* groat, Elizabeth I, 1561, in fine silver.
⑯	**16**. base metal shilling, Elizabeth I, 1558. **17 & 18**. *O.* & *R.* shilling,
⑰ ⑱	James I, 1605, in fine silver. **19**. Inchiquin halfcrown, 1642. **20**. *O.*
⑲	Ormonde halfcrown, 1643. **21**. *R.*
⑳ ㉑	Ormonde shilling, 1643. All reduced in size.

22, 23 & 24. St Patrick's halfpennies, 1670s. 25. *R*. halfpenny, Charles II, 1680. 26. *O*. halfpenny, James II, 1685. All at natural size.

Inchiquin crowns and halfcrowns and other denominations bearing symbols indicating their weight and hence their value, were crudely struck from silver plate (**19**). Other siege pieces include the so-called Dublin money, Ormonde money and the Blacksmith's halfcrown, all fashioned from silver plate. The Ormonde series (**20** and **21**) ranges from 5*s* to 2*d*, each coin having on one side its value in roman numerals. In 1642 crude halfpennies and farthings were struck in Kilkenny and later four Munster towns, Bandon, Cork, Kinsale and Youghal, struck their own coins, those for shillings and sixpences for Cork being of silver. Finally, after the death of Charles in 1649, crowns and halfcrowns were struck in Dublin to a similar (Ormonde) design for Charles II.

The circumstances of the next issue is in some doubt but it was probably produced in Dublin *c.* 1674. St Patrick's halfpennies and farthings have on the obverse St Patrick preaching in front of a cathedral and on the reverse King David playing a harp, with a crown above (**22** to **24**). These coins were taken in large quantities to America, where they are regarded as part of the USA pre-independence coinage, as well as to the Isle of Man, where they circulated legally as currency.

After the Restoration of Charles II the shortage of regal coinage caused many merchants and towns to issue their own tokens and these circulated freely over a wide area of Ireland. About 800 distinct tokens are known covering 170 cities, towns and villages and all counties except Mayo. Dublin was responsible for the issue of over 170 varieties by 145 issuers. Most of these tokens for a penny were fashioned from thin pieces of copper and usually give the name or initials of the issuer and sometimes an indication of his trade.

Regal halfpennies bearing the bust of Charles II on one side and a crowned harp on the other (**25**) were issued in 1680–4, followed in 1685–8 by similar halfpennies struck for James II (**26**).

In 1601–2 small thin copper pennies and halfpennies having the royal arms on one side and a harp on the other were minted for Elizabeth. James I's issues in silver included shillings (**17** and **18**) and sixpences, all with the harp reverse. From 1613 farthings were issued under royal licence, with crown and sceptre on the obverse and a crowned harp on the reverse. Similar farthings were again issued for Charles I. There were no other regal issues but siege money was struck in 1642–6, including the only gold issued for Ireland, the Inchiquin double pistoles and pistoles (**122** to **124**), issued in 1646.

James II abdicated in 1688 and fled to France but in 1689 he came to Ireland in an attempt to regain his throne. On arrival in Ireland he found a scarcity of coin. He established mints in Dublin and Limerick to strike sixpences (**27** and **28**), shillings (**29** and **30**) and halfcrowns (**32** and **33**) in brass and base metal, mainly obtained from old cannons, hence the common name for this coinage – *gunmoney*. Later when metal became scarce the shillings (**31**) and halfcrowns (**34**) were reduced in size, and many of the halfcrowns were restruck as crowns (**35** and **36**).

The designs of all the sixpences, shillings and halfcrowns were similar, the king's head being on the obverse and a crown and sceptre on the reverse with the denomination (in pennies) in roman numerals, together with the year and month of issue. The reason for the month on these pieces was the declared intention of the king to redeem the coins in good silver in the order of issue when he regained his throne, which, of course, he never did. The crowns have an equestrian portrait of the king holding an upright sword (**36**).

One interesting feature of these coins is that because in the seventeenth century New Year's Day was 25 March, January, February and March 1689 would now belong to 1690.

A few pewter coins were also struck and authorised to pass as pennies and halfpennies and in April 1690 a few white metal crowns were produced but few seem to have circulated.

After the Battle of the Boyne the mint in Dublin was seized by the Williamite forces and gunmoney was reduced to the value of the metal they contained. Finally they were demonetised in 1691. Limerick held out for James and gunmoney bearing dates after July 1690 were minted there. Later gunmoney shillings were restruck as halfpennies and farthings at Limerick. These bear the king's head on the obverse and Hibernia seated with harp on the reverse (**37**). They are dated 1691.

27 & 28. O. & R. of gunmoney sixpence, February, 1689. **29 & 30.** O. & R. of large gunmoney shilling, October, 1689. **31.** O. of small gunmoney shilling. **32 & 33.** O. & R. large gunmoney halfcrown, March 1690. **34.** R. small gunmoney halfcrown. **35 & 36.** O. & R. gunmoney crown (5s), 1690. **37.** R. Limerick halfpenny, 1691. All reduced in size.

Portrait of Dean Swift in St Patrick's Deanery, Dublin.

38 & 39. *O. & R.* Wood's halfpenny, 1723. **40 & 41.** *O. & R.* Wood's farthings, 1723. Slightly enlarged in size.

From 1692 to 1694 regal halfpennies were struck of the type issued for Charles II and James II earlier but with the conjoined busts of William and Mary on the obverse. After Mary's death William's head alone appears on the obverse of the halfpennies issued in 1696. No copper coins were struck for Anne but in 1722 the Duchess of Richmond, George I's mistress, obtained a patent to coin copper money for Ireland, which she subsequently sold to a man named William Wood for £10,000. Wood began to mint halfpennies and farthings at a rate of thirty pence to the pound of metal, which was lighter than the contemporary English copper coins.

From the beginning there was considerable opposition to the coinage in Ireland; the Irish House of Commons, which had not been consulted, petitioning the king against it. Jonathan Swift in his now famous *Drapier's Letters*, poured scorn on the coins and in 1725 Wood resigned his patent and withdrew the coins. Many of the halfpennies and farthings found their way to America.

Despite the opposition to Wood's coinage, the coins (**38 to 41**), dated 1722 to 1724, were not unattractive, having on the obverse the king's head and on the reverse the figure of Hibernia with a harp.

With the withdrawal of Wood's coinage the shortage of small coin became acute. This prompted a number of merchants, mainly in the Ulster counties of Antrim, Armagh, Down, Londonderry and Tyrone, but also two in Dublin, to issue their own tokens. Unlike the earlier seventeenth-century tokens, which were for a penny or a halfpenny, these included pieces for twopence and threepence, some in silver but mainly in copper.

Now halfpennies for George II were struck at the Royal Mint in London in 1736 and for most of the years up to 1755, with farthings for 1737–8 and 1744. These have the laureated bust of the king on the obverse and crowned harp on the reverse.

Halfpennies and farthings were struck for 1760 (**42** and **43**), the king being depicted with older features, but they were not issued until after the king's death in October. In 1760 a Dublin button-maker named Roche had struck a series of halfpennies and farthings with a laureated head (not the king's) on the obverse and a legend Voce Populi (the Voice of the People) (**44**) and Hibernia with a harp on the reverse.

Halfpennies were struck in London in 1766, 1769, 1785–6 and 1791–2, each having the laureated bust of the king on the obverse and the traditional crowned harp on the reverse. Lightweight forgeries of very good workmanship are well known, most having been made in Birmingham. For twenty-three years no regal copper coins were minted for Ireland, but in 1805 pennies (**47**) and halfpennies (**46**) and in 1806 farthings (**45**) were produced at the Soho (Birmingham) mint in fairly large quantities. Because of the accuracy of striking and the engrailed edges, unlike the earlier ones, these coins were difficult to counterfeit.

A marked shortage of regal coins towards the end of the eighteenth century encouraged many mining and other companies in the period 1789–1804 to issue copper tokens, mainly for halfpennies but some farthings. Silver tokens, which are described overleaf, were also issued to alleviate the shortage of regal silver.

A few merchants, mainly in Dublin, but one each in Coleraine and Strabane, issued their own penny and sometimes halfpenny tokens. Many of these have on them a bust of Wellington and others of Edmund Burke and Daniel O'Connell. We also find the Irish motto ERIN GO BRAGH on some of the tokens.

The final coinage of the Anglo-Irish series was issued in the years 1822 and 1823, consisting of pennies (**48**) and halfpennies of a similar design to those issued earlier in the century but with the laureated bust of George IV. From then until 1928 the Imperial coinage was used in Ireland.

42 & 43. *Rs.* halfpenny & farthing, 1760. 44. *R.* Voce Populi halfpenny, 1760. 45, 46 & 47. *Rs.* farthing, halfpenny and penny, 1805. 48. *R.* penny, 1823. All reduced in size.

There was a great shortage of regal silver towards the end of the eighteenth and the beginning of the nineteenth century. Much of the silver was of foreign origin, particularly from Spain and the Americas. In Britain Spanish pieces of eight reales of crown size were countermarked with the king's head and later they were restruck as Bank of England dollars. In Ireland a few pieces of eight were countermarked for Castlecomer in County Kilkenny.

The Bank of Ireland had large numbers of Spanish and Spanish American pieces of eight restruck as six-shilling bank tokens. These have on the obverse the laureated head of George III and on the reverse the figure of Hibernia with harp (49), all being dated 1804. They were produced in Matthew Boulton's mint in Birmingham by a new steam coining press process.

Smaller denomination silver tokens for thirty pence, ten pence and five pence were also issued by the Bank of Ireland about this time. The denominations are given in *pence Irish*, which differed from English pence at the beginning of the nineteenth century, thirteen pence Irish equalling twelve pence English. Each of these tokens has the laureated head of George III (50 and 55). The thirty-pence token (51) has a similar figure of Hibernia to that of the six-shilling token, whereas the ten-pence and five-pence tokens have plain inscriptions (52 to 54).

This series of tokens was extensively counterfeited in a variety of metals. Indeed, the number of forgeries now probably equals those of genuine pieces. Some of the counterfeited tokens were cast in lead or similar base metal but others of the six-shilling denomination were fabricated, mainly in Birmingham, in an ingenious way. Two genuine pieces were taken; the obverse of one and the reverse of the other were ground down to paper thin. These thin pieces bearing the genuine design in silver were soldered on to brass blanks and a silver collar was then put on to hide the brass blank. To make up for the lower density of brass the blank was made slightly thicker than a genuine coin. In this way the counterfeit could not be detected by mere weighing. Apart from the bank

Bank of Ireland tokens. 49. *O.* six shillings, 1804. 50 & 51. thirty pence, 1808. 52. *R.* ten pence, 1805. 53. *R.* ten pence, 1813. 54 & 55. *O.* & *R.* five pence 1805. Slightly reduced in size.

(56) (57) (58)
(59) (60) (61)

56 to **61**. Selection of nineteenth-century advertisement tokens. All greatly enlarged in size.

tokens a number of merchants issued silver tokens for one shilling.

In the middle of last century many publicans provided facilities for games for their customers. As it was illegal to gamble on licensed premises it was usual for the loser or losers to pay for a round of drinks. In this way the publican got some return for his trouble. If a man was winning he might be due more drink than he wanted, so the publican would give him a token, which could be exchanged for drink in future. Many Irish hostelries had their own special tavern tokens, as they were called, most being designed by the Irish medallist, Isaac Parkes, of the Coombe, a part of ancient Dublin.

Up to the Second World War drapers and similar firms seldom priced their goods in whole shillings but reduced the price by one farthing so they charged $11\frac{3}{4}d$, rather than $1s$, $9/11\frac{3}{4}d$ and not $10s$. But in the middle of last century regal farthings were not plentiful so many firms had farthing advertisement tokens struck to facilitate trade. Many of the tokens were of the same size as the early Victorian British farthing and many actually had the Queen's head on one side of the token (**56** to **61**). Most of the tokens have the name, and sometimes the address of the issuer, often with some device indicating his trade (**58**). Ornaments such as shamrocks and harps (**57**) were not uncommon nor was the symbolic rose, thistle and shamrock on the same stem (**61**). These tokens were issued by over a hundred firms located in thirty-nine towns, and many bear the imprint of John Craig Parkes of the Coombe, Dublin.

Possession of a distinctive coinage is a sure sign of nationhood so it was not surprising that in 1926 the government of the Irish Free State should have decided to introduce new coins to supersede those of Great Britain, which had circulated as legal tender in Ireland for over a hundred years. An expert committee, under the chairmanship of the well-known poet and writer, William Butler Yeats, was set up by the Government to advise on designs for new coins and a number of artists were invited to submit proposals for the new coinage. After much deliberation the committee decided upon the designs of Percy Metcalf, a British medallist, who had done much work for the Royal Mint in London. The Irish Government accepted the advice given and a contract was placed with the Royal Mint for eight denominations of coins, similar to those of Britain and most of the same size, and dated 1928.

The obverse of all denominations consists of a harp with the date and a legend SAORSTÁT ÉIREANN, as shown on the outer flap. The reverse had the image of some animal and an indication of the denomination in Irish and in figures. The animals were a horse for the halfcrown, a salmon for the florin or two shillings, a bull for the shilling, a greyhound for the sixpence, a hare for the threepence, a chicken with chicks for the penny, a sow with piglets for the halfpenny and a woodcock for the smallest coin, the farthing. The obverse of the 1928 halfcrown and the reverses of all the denominations are shown on the flap. Silver (75 per cent) was used for the three largest coins, cupro-nickel for the shilling and six-pence, and bronze for the three smallest coins.

In 1937 a new constitution was enacted and the name of the state was changed in Irish to ÉIRE. This necessitated a change in the coinage, the name ÉIRE being substituted for SAORSTÁT ÉIREANN (as shown in the illustration on the halfcrown of 1942 on the outer flap). The former silver denominations were produced in cupro-nickel from 1951 onwards.

A commemorative ten-shilling piece was issued for the Jubilee of the 1916 Rising with on the obverse the bust of Padraic Pearse, one of the executed leaders, and on the reverse a statue of Cuchulainn and an edge inscription in Irish.

When decimalisation was introduced in 1971 the traditional harp obverses were retained. Three of the older reverse designs were retained for those of the 50p (woodcock), 10p (salmon) and 5p (bull) but new designs, derived from old Irish manuscripts, were introduced for 2p, 1p and ½p (as shown on the outer flap).

62 & 63. O. & R. of 6d truck ticket, Ballyglunin. **64 & 65**. O. & R. 2s 6d truck ticket, G. W. Stewart. **66**. 6d ticket, Blake, Menlough. Natural size.

It is now usual to pay workmen in official currency, but for a very long period many employers paid their workforce at least part of their wages in the form of specially struck 'coins' which could only be used in the shops of their employers or those with whom the employers had made arrangements to cash the so-called truck tickets. This led to a great deal of abuse and many attempts were made to prohibit the practice by a series of Acts of Parliament, known colloquially as *The Truck Acts*. However, many of the former truck tickets used in Ireland still survive, indicating how widespread was the practice. Many of these truck tickets were well struck and designed. M. J. Blake of Ballyglunin, County Galway, had a series of such tickets ranging in value from a halfpenny to eight pence (**62** and **63**). G. W. Stewart of Lisdourt had three tickets dated 1867 for halfcrown (**64** and **65**), shilling and penny. Another Blake of Menlough, near Galway, had a fine truck ticket

with a leopard on its reverse (**66**).

A lack of Irish gold and large silver coins over a long period meant that continental foreign coins circulated freely in Ireland. In order to determine the value of a particular coin in Irish currency a merchant would weigh it and then consult a table setting out the Irish equivalent of the more prominent coins. To facilitate weighing, coin weights, each bearing its weight in pennyweights and grains, were produced in Ireland, authorised by official proclamations. Many of these coin weights display a harp (**68** to **71**, and **73**), often with the legend STANDARD OF IRELAND, and some have the regal arms (**72**). Irish coin weights are known from 1632 until early in the nineteenth century. In the selection of the coin weights illustrated below (**67** to **73**) there are those for a half French louis d'or (**68**), Spanish and French pistole (**69**), a 'new' (1737) French louis d'or (**70**), Portuguese moidre (**71**) and double pistole (**72**). Later coin weights were made in Ireland during the first half of the nineteenth century for gold coins, including sovereigns and half-sovereigns.

67 to **73**. A selection of Irish coin weights. All enlarged in size.

74. Military Medal for Gallantry. 75. Scott Medal. 76. Black and Tan Medal. 77. 1916 Medal. 78. 1916 Survivors Medal. 79. 1921 Survivors Medal.

80. 15-year Service Medal. 81. Emergency Service Medal, 1939–46. 82. 10-year Service Medal. 83. Reserve Defence Force Medal. All reduced in size.

84. Merchant Marine Medal, 1939–46. **85, 86 & 87**. Distinguished Service Medals, First Class, Third Class & Second Class, respectively. **88 & 89**. St John Ambulance Brigade Medals. **90 & 91**. Order of Malta Ambulance Corps Medals. **92 & 93**. Irish Red Cross Society Medals. **94 & 95**. Commissioners of Irish Lights Medals. All reduced in size.

For centuries the courage of Irishmen who joined the armies of Britain and other countries has been rewarded with foreign military honours, in the case of the British Army including the coveted Victoria Cross. In recent years members of the Irish army have been awarded medals of the United Nations Organisation in connection with peace-keeping activities in the Congo, Cyprus and the Middle East. Although a separate Irish State had been established much earlier, it was not until the year 1941, on the Silver Jubilee of the 1916 Rising, that the Irish Government instituted the first genuine Irish military medal (77) for award to those who took part in the Easter Week Rising. This medal takes precedence over other Irish medals. Instituted at the same time was the Service Medal for 1917–21 (76), awarded to those who took part in operations against the British forces from 1917 to 1921. This medal, colloquially known as the Black and Tan medal, an allusion to the mixed uniform of members of the British forces, ranks second in precedence in Irish military medals.

In 1944 the Irish Government instituted what is now the rarest of the Irish military awards, the Military Medal for Gallantry (74). This medal has only been awarded once and that posthumously to Trooper Anthony Browne, who in 1966 stayed with a wounded comrade until his post was overrun and he was later killed in the Niembe ambush in the Congo. Also in 1944 the Irish Government instituted a Service medal for members of the Defence Forces. This was awarded for ten years' service (82), with a bar for fifteen years' service (80).

Troops of the Irish army have been engaged in peace-keeping and other duties under the United Nations in several parts of the world and in 1964 the Irish Government decided to institute the Distinguished Service Medal in recognition of conduct of a very high order but not meriting the award of the Military Medal for Gallantry. Distinguished Service Medals are issued in three classes, First Class (85), Second Class (87) and Third Class (86).

The Jubilee of 1916 was celebrated in 1966 and another award, the Survivors Medal, was presented to those persons who, having taken part in the 1916 Rising, survived until 1966 (78).

The 'Emergency', an Irish euphemism for the Second World War, saw the institution of a series of medals for award to those who served for a qualifying period. The medals were issued in two divisions, one for the regular and auxiliary forces and one for the civilian support forces. There are eleven different reverses and two patterns of ribbons, that for the regular forces being shown in 81. A Merchant Marine Medal (84) was also instituted in 1944 for those who served on board an Irish registered merchant ship during the Emergency. A Service Medal was instituted in 1961 for those members of the Army and Naval reserve forces, who had served seven years continuously, with a bar for an additional five years (83).

The highly prized Scott medal was the brainchild of Walter Scott, a wealthy Canadian, who provided funds for the purpose. It is awarded in gold (75), silver and bronze on the recommendation of the Commissioner to members of the Garda Siochana (Police) for deeds of exceptional bravery and courage.

Civil Medals for Bravery were instituted in 1947 in two classes, gold and bronze, for award to persons other than those in the Defence Forces. Other organisations have issued special medals. They include the Irish Red Cross (the President's Medal (92) and the Medal of Merit (93)), the St John Ambulance Brigade of Ireland (Service Medals for fifteen years (89) and fifty years (88)), the Order of Malta Ambulance Corps (Merit (90) and Service (91) medals), and the Irish Lights Commission (94 and 95).

Medals, medallions and medallets

have been used for many centuries elsewhere in the world to commemorate notable events and personalities but, possibly because of her history, Ireland was late in this field and it was not until late in the eighteenth century that many such medals were produced in Ireland. William Mossop, a Dublin-born self-taught man, in the last quarter of that century, started to strike fine medals for a variety of purposes. His finest work is undoubtedly the Cunningham medal of the Royal Irish Academy (shown on the front cover) awarded in gold on thirty-five occasions. The obverse shows the bust of James, Earl of Charlemont, first president of the Academy, in the uniform of an officer of the Irish Volunteers. Mossop's portrait medals were said to be good likenesses. They include those for Dr Henry Quin, Mossop's benefactor, Edmund Sexton, Viscount Pery, Speaker of the Irish House of Commons from 1771 to 1785, William Deane (**96**), a Dublin solicitor, distinguished in many scientific activities, William Alexander, Lord Mayor of Dublin in 1788 and David La Touche (**97**), the famous Dublin banker, Thomas Ryder, the famous Irish actor, and Richard Robinson, Lord Rokeby (**98**), who, as Archbishop of Armagh, used his personal fortune to improve the capital city of his archdiocese.

Mossop did not restrict himself to portrait medals but produced others including those for Trinity College, Dublin (**141**), the Friendly Brothers of St Patrick, the Bantry Bay Association (**105**), the Masonic Order, the Farming Society of Ireland, the Navan Farming Society, the Dublin Society (now the Royal Dublin Society), the Irish Ordnance (**108**) and the Orange Order (**151**). Many of the well-known 'Camac' halfpenny tokens issued from 1789 onwards in Ireland were designed by Mossop. A tiny medal commemorating Dean Jonathan Swift has been attributed to Mossop. Apart from his Irish medals Mossop struck a number of medals in the 1790s commemorating Marie-Antoinette, Louis XVI of France and other French personages.

William Stephen Mossop (1751–1805).

96. William Deane, 1785. **97**. David La Touche, 1785. **98**. Richard Robinson, Lord Rokeby, 1789.

99. Hibernia restored, 1691. 100. Surplus Revenue Dispute, 1753. 101. Louth Election, 1755. 102. Act of Union, 1800. 103. Belfast Unionist Convention. All reduced in size.

Political and historical medals are not uncommon in the Irish series. Some of the earliest relate to William III (99). Surplus revenue in the Irish Exchequer in 1753 had given rise to heated disputes when the Crown claimed that it, and not the Irish Parliament, had the right to decide on its disposal. Several medals were struck to commemorate the dispute, the commonest has on one side a crowned harp (100) and on the other an inscription, 'Touch not says Kildare', an allusion to the Earl of Kildare's opposition to the Crown's claim. A successful attempt to oust a local magnate from Parliament in a Louth election is commemorated by a medal by Pingo (101). The Act of Union in 1800 was the subject of many medals, one by Hancock (102) being quite common. A Unionist Convention in Belfast in 1892, which had important political results, was the subject of a medal (103).

The destruction of the French fleet off Bantry Bay in 1796 (105) and the Battle of Collooney, in which the Limerick Militia was engaged against the French (106), were the subject of medals by William Mossop and James Brush. Another medal by an unknown artist was presented by the Corporation of Waterford to those engaged in the city's defence in 1798 (107). William Stephen Mossop, son of William Mossop, produced a fine medal dated 1814 (104) for the Apprentice Boys of Derry, depicting the apprentice boys shutting the gates in the face of James II's troops. The reverse of this medal has the facing bust of George Walker, the defender of Derry during the siege. The Irish Ordnance, later merged with the Royal Artillery, had silver and bronze medals designed by Mossop Senior (108).

104. Apprentice Boys of Derry, 1814. 105. Bantry Bay Association, 1797. 106. Battle of Collooney, 1798. 107. Waterford Defence Medal, 1799. 108. Irish Ordnance Medal. All reduced in size.

109 & 110. Daniel O'Connell. 111. William Dargan. 112. Charles Stewart Parnell. 113. William Ewart Gladstone. All enlarged in size.

William Mossop was the first Irish artist to strike portrait medals, some of which have been mentioned earlier. His portrait of William III (151) produced c. 1797 is particularly good. William's son, William Stephen Mossop, also produced a number of fine portrait medals and that of Henry Grattan was intended to be the first of a series to commemorate forty illustrious Irishmen, but only the Grattan medal was completed.

No Irishman was the subject of more medals and medallets than Daniel O'Connell, many being struck immediately after his death in 1847 and again when the monument to his memory was erected in the centre of Dublin (109 and 110).

Isaac Parkes and William Woodhouse produced medals depicting Irishmen concerned with a wide range of activities. For example, Woodhouse produced a medal, sold at the Great Industrial Exhibition in Dublin in 1853, which had on it the bust of William Dargan (111) who financed the event.

Later Parnell, at times on his own, but on others with Gladstone (112 and 113), was the subject of many brass medallets. Nearer our own time we have medals issued in 1966, to celebrate the Jubilee of the 1916 Rising, with a portrait of Padraic Pearse (158) and in more recent years medals were struck to commemorate Eamon de Valera (159), former President of Ireland. The latest of the de Valera medals were struck, as is now quite customary, in platinum, gold, silver and bronze.

Ireland can be justly proud of its agricultural and farming society medals, some of which are shown on the inner flap on the front cover. Pre-eminent among these organisations was the Dublin Society, which, founded in 1731 'for improving husbandry, manufactures and other useful arts and sciences', issued its first medals in 1763. From 1763 to 1768 medals were issued only in gold but from then onwards silver and bronze medals were issued. Those taking part in various competitions with '£500 a year in landed property or £10,000 personal estate' were by by-laws debarred from receiving cash premiums but instead they would be awarded a gold medal, if the premium was £10 or more, or a silver medal if less. The first medal was used from 1763 (**114**) until c. 1804, when a new oval medal by William Mossop was substituted for it. Mossop's medal was used until about 1824, and was then replaced by a circular medal by Mossop Junior. Re-engravings of Mossop's medal were later made firstly by George Brown and later by Isaac Parkes for use in the years 1835 until 1845. Parkes himself produced in 1842 a circular medal, similar to that of Mossop Junior, and a second medal of quite similar design was also designed by Isaac Parkes but bearing the imprint of his son J. C. Parkes. From 1847 William Woodhouse produced a series of new medals having on the reverse five breeds of cattle, a cow and calf, and a mare and foal. John Woodhouse, son of William Woodhouse, produced from 1860 a series of fine medals, the trotting horse design being particularly attractive. In 1892 a new design of medal by an unknown artist was introduced and this was used until 1930. To celebrate the bicentenary of the Society in 1931 a re-engraving of Mossop's 1804 medal was introduced and this is still in use today.

The Farming Society of Ireland, founded in 1800, for many years carried out many activities aimed at encouraging agricultural and farming pursuits. Its medal by William Mossop was issued for a number of years but gradually it became obvious that the Society was duplicating activities already performed by the Royal Dublin Society so the two societies merged. Another society, the Agricultural Improvement Society of Ireland, was established in 1841, also to encourage agricultural and farming pursuits, by holding an annual agricultural show and supporting local farming societies by providing medals. Later the Society obtained royal patronage and medals by William Woodhouse and later by John Jones were struck for its purposes. When in 1860 the Society received its royal charter it dropped the word Improvement from its title and from 1861 until it was merged with the Royal Dublin Society, medals by John Jones and John Woodhouse were issued for shows over almost the whole of Ireland.

Isaac Parkes was a prolific producer of agricultural society and farming society medals. All his animals are well displayed and he frequently included farm machinery, such as ploughs, in the designs. But what was particularly distinctive in Parkes's designs were the farm buildings in the background, often with human figures tending the farm stock. A good example of Parkes's work is the medal for the Roscommon Agriculture Society. Standard designs were often used on one side of the medals, the reverse only having the name of the individual society with some type of decoration or other.

Among the other Irish artists producing agricultural and farming society medals were William Woodhouse and his son John. British artists had, however, over a long period produced such medals, good examples being those by C. R. Collis for the Roscommon Union Agricultural Society and J. Moore for the North Kildare Farming Society. The Belfast counterpart of the Royal Dublin Society in Dublin is the Royal Ulster Agricultural Society, which, with its predecessor the North

East Agricultural Association of Ireland, had fine medals produced by Jarrett of London for use in connection with its shows.

Gold medals, except for Trinity College, Dublin (116, 117 and 140 etc.), are not particularly common in the Irish series, the rarest probably being the early medals of the Dublin Society (114) and those of Father Mathew's temperance societies (120). Medals in gold were struck for the Jubilee of the 1916 Rising and Eamon de Valera (158 and 159) and Ireland's accession to the EEC in 1973 (118).

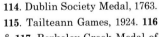

114. Dublin Society Medal, 1763. 115. Tailteann Games, 1924. 116 & 117. Berkeley Greek Medal of Trinity College, Dublin. 118. Ireland's Accession to EEC, 1973. 119. Clongowes Wood, School Medal. 120. Father Mathew Medal, 1840. 121. University College, Dublin, Medal. 122. Inchiquin double pistole. 123 & 124. O. & R. of Inchiquin pistoles.

125. Cork Total Abstinence Society. 126 & 127. O. & R. Total Abstinence Society of Ireland. 128. Father Mathew O.S.F. Total Abstinence Association. 129. Irish Total Abstinence Ass. 130. Irish Protestant Abstinence Society. Sizes reduced.

In the early part of last century many people interested in the welfare of Irish men and women were greatly concerned at the intemperate habits of a high proportion of the population. Drunkenness was rife and to combat this temperance or total abstinence societies were established in many places. Pre-eminent among those concerned was Father Theobald Mathew, a member of the Capuchin Order who, for a period of just under twenty years from 10 April 1838 until his death on 8 December 1856, gave the pledge to many thousands of grateful men and women at ceremonies all over Ireland, and indeed, in Britain and America as well. Even if many of the contemporary accounts of Father Mathew's conversions exaggerate the actual numbers who took the pledge, nevertheless the numbers must have been considerable. Ordinary members of the public would receive medals in white metal or brass, whereas a priest or other V.I.P. would receive a silver medal, a few only being presented in gold to very special people. The commonest design of medal has on its obverse figures of a man and a woman, standing around a set of arms with two small children at their feet and holding flags in their arms. The man's flag bears the word 'Sobriety' and the woman's 'Domestic Happiness' (125). On the reverse is the pledge, surrounded by the name of the issuing Society. The usual pledge reads, 'I promise to abstain from all intoxicating drinks etc. except used medicinally and by order of a medical man and to discountenance the cause and practice of intemperance' (127). Other medals have on the obverse the figure of St Patrick casting out the snakes (126), Father Mathew's bust (128) or a crucifix (129).

Mention has already been made of gold medals (120) presented by Father Mathew. Very few such medals are known. A Mrs O'Reilly was presented with a gold medal, valued at £5, in return for the hospitality she and her husband showed when Father Mathew stayed with them in November 1840. Three other such medals are known to have been presented to the Most Rev. John Hughes, Archbishop of New York in 1849, the Most Rev. Dr Foran, Bishop of Waterford and to a Rev. Dr John Miley, who appears to have been a priest attached to the Pro-Cathedral in Dublin.

Protestant organisations also issued temperance medals (130), but most of these have no pledge, or one very much reduced in length.

Pupils at many Irish schools in days long gone by were exceedingly keen on the medals for which they were eligible and many fine medals were offered for award, none finer than the gold medal of Clongowes College (**119**). However, the Clongowes medal was exceptional, most Irish school medals being of silver or occasionally bronze. The King's Hospital, formerly known as the Blue-Coat School, founded in Dublin in 1670, in the last century had a fine medal with a stylised view of the building in which the school was housed for many years until recently (**131**). Royal schools established in Armagh, Cavan, Enniskillen and Raphoe all had their distinctive medals, that of Raphoe by Woodhouse, having a mitre and the school's motto on the obverse (**132**), being a particularly fine medal. Dungannon, another Royal school, used a standard school medal by Pingo (**133**), an English medallist, with a special engraving of the name of the recipient, etc. on the reverse.

Schools in Drogheda, Dublin, Ennis, Galway and Tipperary, established as a result of the benefactions of an Englishman, Erasmus Smith, at first used engraved medals but later used a standard medal for all schools (**134** and **135**) each being especially engraved with the name of the school, and of the recipient, etc. Many private schools of former days would hardly be remembered now but for the existence of these medals. For example, a finishing school for young ladies in Kildare Place, Dublin, in a building demolished for twenty years, had a small medal by Woodhouse for presentation to its pupils. The Rev. Benson's Rathmines School, the former pupils of which in after life filled many important offices in Church and State in Ireland and abroad, had two regular school medals (**136** and **137**), and Mossop's school medal (**139**) was widely used by other schools in Ireland.

The Royal Hibernian Military School in Dublin, which has now disappeared,

131. King's Hospital, Dublin. **132**. Raphoe Royal School. **133**. Dungannon Royal School. **134 & 135**. O. & R. Erasmus Smith Schools. **136 & 137**. Rev. Benson's School, Rathmines (Dublin). **138**. Royal Hibernian Military School. **139**. Armagh & Connor Diocesan School. All reduced in size.

had a medal with a crowned harp on its obverse (**138**) for presentation to the young aspiring army men. Irish and other medallists concerned certainly used all their talents in particularly fine school medals for Ireland.

Trinity College, Dublin, Medal
(1868).

140 to **142**, **145**, **147** and **148**.
Medals of Trinity College, Dublin
(various dates). **143**. Mater Hospital, Dublin, Medical Medal.
144. Jervis Street Hospital, Dublin. **146 & 149**, Carmichael Medal
of Royal College of Surgeons in
Ireland. **150**. Sir Patrick Duns
Hospital, Dublin. All reduced in
size.

Trinity College, Dublin, leads the seats
of higher education with the number of
medals it has issued over a long period
of time. Most of the medals have the
bust of the College's founder, Queen
Elizabeth I (**142** and **145**). On the 300th
anniversary of the foundation of the
College, a fine medal was issued with
the conjoined busts of Elizabeth I and
Victoria (**147**). During the First World
War patriotic former students who
handed in their gold medals were given
a bronze replica (**148**). Special medals
for Classics and Greek (**116** and **117**) in
gold were issued by the College. Much
sought after medals are those issued by
the Historical Society, the earliest from
the end of the eighteenth century (**140**)
being by an unknown artist and
another by William Mossop (**141**). Most
of the medical schools in Ireland
present medals for various subjects
(**143–4**, **146**, **149** and **150**) and the
institution concerned with engineering
has medals for award to distinguished
engineers, who have produced papers at
its meetings.

The Orange Order was established towards the end of the eighteenth century and was a powerful force, particularly in the province of Ulster. Its objects were to commemorate and maintain the Protestant supremacy in Church and State as established by the Battle of the Boyne. In view of its importance in religious and political affairs it is not surprising that Orange Order medals should have been produced in abundance, especially at the end of the eighteenth and the first half of the nineteenth century. Mossop Senior and James Brush were the first Irish artists to design and strike medals for the Order. Mossop's medal (**151**) has on its obverse a bust of William III with the legend THE GLORIOUS & IMMORTAL MEMORY 1690 and on the reverse the royal arms with the words KING AND CONSTITUTION above. James Brush, whose Collooney medal (**106**) has already been mentioned, produced two Orange Order medals, one oval and one circular. Brush's designs are rather crude, the circular medal having an equestrian figure of the king on the obverse (**152**) with a legend THE GLORIOUS MEMORY / KING AND CONSTITUTION, with a crown and sceptres on the reverse surrounded by a wreath.

Mossop Junior's medals for the Order are of the same fine quality as those of his father. Again an equestrian figure representing the king is on the obverse (**154**) with the royal arms on the reverse (**155**). The legends on both sides follow those of Mossop Senior.

An equestrian figure based on a statue which was formerly in College Green, Dublin, provided a basis for the obverse of many of Isaac Parkes's medals for the Order. One of the finest has on its reverse a bust of the Duke of York, son of George III, who was a vigorous opponent of relaxation of the disabilities which Roman Catholics suffered. One impression of this medal in a brass frame formed a testimonial to

Selection of Orange Medals. **151.** by William Mossop. **152.** by James Brush. **153.** by John Jones. **154 & 155.** by William Stephen Mossop. **156.** by unknown artist. **157.** by Isaac Parkes. All reduced in size.

a Brother Underwood for services to his Lodge (**157**). John Jones was also a prolific supplier of Orange Order medals but he used mainly Mossop Junior's dies, substituting JONES. F for the name of his erstwhile master (**153**). Other unknown artists also produced Orange Order medals (**156**).

We know little about who designed the early Irish coinage but for some of the hammered pieces we have the moneyer's name only, knowing nothing of him as a person. In the case of medals, medallions or medallets we often have the imprint of the artist, or his initials, to guide us as to their designer, and a high proportion of the finer medals issued from 1780 to 1880 were the work of Irish artists, notably, William Mossop, his son William Stephen Mossop, Isaac Parkes, John Jones, William Woodhouse and his son John.

William Mossop was undoubtedly Ireland's greatest medallist, his finest work being the Cunningham medal of the Royal Irish Academy (shown on the front cover). Born in Dublin in 1751, Mossop was educated at the King's Hospital in Dublin and was later apprenticed to a die-sinker and engraver. He set up business for himself about 1770 and in the 1780s started to produce a fine series of medals, many of which have already been described. He prepared the dies and struck the half-pennies and farthings for the firm of Camac, Kyan and Camac. When that firm failed in 1797 he returned to die-sinking. He died in January 1805, one of his last medals being that for the Dublin Society.

William Stephen Mossop was born in Dublin in 1789 and on the death of his father in 1805 he was thrown on his own resources. About 1820 Mossop produced a medal commemorating Henry Grattan, as part of a contemplated series of forty medals (never completed) of illustrious Irishmen. He made seals for a number of Irish bodies and medals covering a wide range of subjects, some of which have already been described.

Isaac Parkes was born in Birmingham about 1791 and in 1807 he was apprenticed to his brother, then a button-maker. Afterwards he set up in business for himself as a die-sinker, etc. Parkes produced his first medal about 1814. The high relief and quality of his Duke of York medallion was very highly commended and rightly so, as were his long series of medals for many varied organisations, such as temperance societies, schools and agricultural societies. Apart from medals he struck penny tokens for Edward Bewley and Edward Stephens in the period 1812–16, a wide range of advertisement and tavern tokens, used in the middle of last century in Irish hostelries.

Little is known of **John Jones**, except that he was employed by Mossop Junior and that he struck many medals from Mossop's dies, sometimes even substituting his own name. He produced a large number of medals for the Orange Order, temperance societies and for the Royal Agricultural Improvement Society and the Royal Agricultural Society of Ireland (see inside flap).

William Woodhouse was born in Dublin in 1805 and educated there. Later he was apprenticed to Halliday, a well-known medallist in Birmingham, and while there he was awarded the Duke of York's prize for a head of Byron. Said to have been a successful athlete, boxer and horseman, Woodhouse returned to Dublin about 1825 and commenced to cut seals and strike medals for a wide range of schools, exhibitions, societies, including the Royal Dublin Society (see inside flap), and Irish personalities. He ceased to work in the late 1840s and died in 1878 aged seventy-three years, after many years in retirement.

John Woodhouse was also born in Dublin in 1835 and he was trained at the Art School of the Royal Dublin Society. In 1862 he obtained a Prize Medal of the Royal Hibernian Academy for modelling and the following year he was elected as an Associate Academician. He designed many fine medals, for schools, colleges, hospitals, and especially the trotting horse design of the Royal Dublin Society (see flap). In 1885 he prepared a new die for the Cunningham medal (originally designed by William Mossop) for the Royal Irish Academy. He died in May 1892.